God's DAILY ANSWER

devotions to renew your soul

for Graduates

God's
DAILY
ANSWER

---

devotions to renew your soul

---

for Graduates

God is inscrutable—there will always be aspects of His person we aren't capable of understanding. But He knows our need for answers and has responded by giving us the Scriptures, rich oral traditions, and the witness of our hearts to let us know what we can expect from Him, how He wishes to interact with us, and the various aspects of His character. He encourages us to ask, seek, and find.

As you graduate from this phase of your life and move on to new responsibilities and opportunities, you probably have many questions. If so, *God's Daily Answer for Graduates* was designed for you. As you read, you will hear what God has to say about the issues you will be facing in the course of your everyday life—topics like decision making, confidence, family, work, and finances. We hope you will also come to know more intimately the One who holds *all* the answers—the One who holds you in the palm of His hand.

Table of Contents

SEE THAT YOU SET BEFORE YOU
what is truly a high ideal. I do not mean by this
a picture of enormous wealth, of a succession
of pleasures, of high fame coming from
a thousand tongues. Set your heart on something
which cannot be taken from you, something
independent of time, place, and circumstances,
something descending from above, but abiding
within you and which will stay with you.

~

JAMES MCCOSH

Freedom and Independence

Where the Spirit of the Lord is, there is freedom.
2 CORINTHIANS 3:17 NIV

GRADUATION day could be renamed "independence day." It feels like a fresh taste of freedom. The choices and changes that are right around the corner seem a little sweeter than in years past, because the direction you choose to go is solely up to you—and God.

Being dependent on God doesn't interfere with that newfound freedom. Relying on God for guidance, strength, comfort, wisdom, and countless other gifts allows you to risk throwing yourself wholeheartedly into the adventure of life. It's like having a partner belay your rope while rock climbing. It gives you the freedom and courage to tackle higher and harder climbs. The closer the "partnership" you have with God, the freer you'll find you are to reach your true potential.

~~~~~~~~~~~~~~~~~~~~~~~~~~~~~

God forces no one, for love cannot compel,
and God's service, therefore,
is a thing of perfect freedom.

HANS DENCK

Freedom means I have been set free to become
all that God wants me to be, to achieve
all that God wants me to achieve, to enjoy
all that God wants me to enjoy.

WARREN W. WIERSBE

He who trusts in himself is lost.
He who trusts in God can do all things.

SAINT ALPHONSUS LIGUORI

The only lasting treasure is spiritual;
the only perfect freedom is serving God.

MALCOLM MUGGERIDGE

Jesus said, "If the Son makes you free,
you shall be free indeed.

JOHN 8:36 NKJV

Decisions

*If you need wisdom—if you want to know
what God wants you to do—ask him,
and he will gladly tell you.*

JAMES 1:5 NLT

WHEN you're faced with a tough decision, it's only natural to go to a friend for advice. Chatting openly with someone who knows you and your situation well can help you put the pros and cons of your options into clearer perspective. So, what could make more sense than spending time talking things over with the One who knows you better than anyone else?

God cares about the direction in which your life is headed. The decisions you make each day help determine that direction. Weighing your decisions by what's written in the Bible and using the wisdom God provides for the asking will not only help you determine right from wrong, but better from best.

~~~~~~~~~~~~~~~~~~~~~~~~~~~~~~

We make our decisions, and then our decisions turn around and make us.

FRANCIS BOREHAM

God always gives his very best to those
who leave the choice with him.

JAMES HUDSON TAYLOR

Living is a constant process of deciding
what we are going to do.

JOSÉ ORTEGA Y GASSET

We must make the choices that enable us
to fulfill the deepest capacity of our real selves.

THOMAS MERTON

I bless the LORD who gives me counsel;
in the night also my heart instructs me.

PSALM 16:7 NRSV

Growth

*See that you go on growing in the Lord,
and become strong and vigorous in
the truth you were taught.*

COLOSSIANS 2:7 TLB

ONCE you graduate, your place in the world changes. You're finally considered a grown-up, or at least regarded as approaching that designation. But being "grown" doesn't mean you stop growing. Every single day of your life, from the moment you were conceived until the day you meet Jesus face-to-face, you're growing into who God created you to be.

Just like any thriving plant—or person—how well you grow is partially dependent on the quality of the soil you're planted in. When you're firmly rooted in what God has to say about you, you can withstand any type of weather. So, when the storms start to blow, dig down deep into what you know is true.

~~~~~~~~~~~~~~~~~~~~~~~~~~~~~

Be not afraid of growing slowly;
be afraid only of standing still.

A PROVERB

Gradual growth in grace, knowledge, faith, love,
holiness, humility, and spiritual-mindedness—
all this I see clearly taught and urged in Scripture.

J. C. RYLE

Progress in the Christian life is exactly equal to
the growing knowledge we gain of
the Triune God in personal experience.

A. W. TOZER

If we don't change, we don't grow.
If we don't grow, we are not really living.
Growth demands a temporary surrender
of security.

GAIL SHEEHY

We must grow up in every way into him
who is the head, into Christ.

EPHESIANS 4:15 NRSV

Honesty

The LORD hates cheating, but he delights in honesty.
PROVERBS 11:1 NLT

You don't have to be on the FBI's Most Wanted List to be dishonest. All you have to do is exaggerate a personal story to make yourself look better in your friends' eyes. Eat a few grapes before you pay for the bunch at the grocery store. Or record your weight a few pounds lower than reality on a health insurance form.

Dishonesty is a habit that's easy to develop. Honesty is not so easy, but it is a gift to the God who loves you. It tells Him He can trust you. It tells you you can trust yourself. Honesty may stir up some waves on the surface of your life, but deep down in the depths of your soul, it produces genuine, lasting peace.

~~~~~~~~~~~~~~~~~~~~~~~~~~~~~~

Honesty is the first chapter in the book of wisdom.
<div align="right">THOMAS JEFFERSON</div>

Honesty has a beautiful and refreshing
simplicity about it. No ulterior motives.
No hidden meanings.

CHARLES R. SWINDOLL

I consider the most enviable of all titles,
the character of an honest man.

GEORGE WASHINGTON

If we be honest with ourselves,
we shall be honest with each other.

GEORGE MACDONALD

An honest answer is as pleasing as a kiss on the lips.

PROVERBS 24:26 NCV

God's Love

Your constant love reaches above the heavens;
your faithfulness touches the skies.

PSALM 108:4 GNT

"I LOVE YOU" is a phrase everyone longs to hear. However, real love is evident without a word having to be said. It's seen in the attention, affection, and sacrifice people show for the ones they care about.

If you want to know how much God loves you, just look at what He's done. When Jesus died on the cross, He was saying "I love you" more beautifully than it's ever been said before. But God's love didn't stop there. He listens to your prayers as if you were the only person in the world. He brings good things into your life, even out of seemingly impossible situations. God's love for you will not end. Your awareness of that love will grow deeper as you grow closer to Him.

~~~~~~~~~~~~~~~~~~~~~~~~~~~~~

God soon turns from his wrath,
but he never turns from his love.

CHARLES HADDON SPURGEON

God's love is always supernatural,
always a miracle,
always the last thing we deserve.

ROBERT HORN

Jesus did not come to make God's love possible,
but to make God's love visible.

AUTHOR UNKNOWN

Every existing thing is equally upheld
in its existence by God's creative love.

SIMONE WEIL

*God's love has been poured into our hearts through
the Holy Spirit that has been given to us.*

ROMANS 5:5 NRSV

Patience

Be still before the LORD and wait patiently for him.
PSALM 37:7 NIV

WAITING at a red light can drive you nuts. It seems like wasted time—especially if you happen to be in a hurry. But life is filled with metaphorical red lights. Some of them God puts right in front of you on purpose—to slow you down, so you'll wait on Him.

Waiting for God's "green light" in any situation teaches you patience. It reminds you that some things are simply out of your control. It prompts you to stay close in prayer. It protects you by giving you time to mature. It opens your eyes to things you might have missed in your hurry to move further and faster down the road of life. As you're waiting patiently, God is working purposefully.

~~~~~~~~~~~~~~~~~~~~~~~~~~~~~~

Be patient with everyone, but above all, with yourself.
SAINT FRANCIS DE SALES

He who possesses patience, possesses himself.

RAYMOND LULL

Teach us, O Lord, the disciplines of patience,
for to wait is often harder than to work.

PETER MARSHALL

Be patient toward all that is unsolved
in your heart.

DAG HAMMARSKJÖLD

Be patient when trouble comes.
Pray at all times.

ROMANS 12:12 NCV

Wisdom

Wisdom is a tree of life to those who embrace her;
happy are those who hold her tightly.

PROVERBS 3:18 NLT

You don't have to be old to be wise. A lot of old people do really stupid things. But then again, so do a lot of young people. Being wise has less to do with age and IQ than with your ability to apply what God has taught you to your everyday life. Application takes thought, prayer, and effort.

But to apply something, first you have to know it. As you read the Bible, ask God to help you understand what His words meant to the people they were originally written for, then for you individually. (A "life application" or study Bible can help.) Then, put what God teaches you into practice. The more you do, the wiser you—and your actions—will become.

~~~~~~~~~~~~~~~~~~~~~~~~~~~~~

Men may acquire knowledge,
but wisdom is a gift direct from God.

BOB JONES

Wisdom is the application of knowledge.

AUTHOR UNKNOWN

Common sense suits itself to the ways of
the world. Wisdom tries to conform
to the ways of heaven.

JOSEPH JOUBERT

Knowledge comes, but wisdom lingers.

ALFRED LORD TENNYSON

The LORD gives wisdom; from his mouth
come knowledge and understanding.

PROVERBS 2:6 NRSV

Compassion

*The LORD is good to all; he has compassion
on all he has made.*

PSALM 145:9 NIV

IMAGINE what it would be like to see the world through God's eyes. How would you feel about the woman in the wheelchair at the grocery store? The neighbor kid who's just found out his folks are getting a divorce? The homeless guy on the park bench?

Seeing individuals the way God does makes you want to put love into action and help. That's compassion kicking in. Compassion doesn't just feel sorry for people, though. It strives to make a positive difference in their lives. So ask God to help you see through His eyes—then to let you know how to help. Even if the only action you can take is to pray, your compassion can make a difference in the world.

~~~~~~~~~~~~~~~~~~~~~~~~~~~~

Man is never nearer the Divine than
in his compassionate moments.

JOSEPH H. HERTZ

Man may dismiss compassion from his heart,
but God will never.

WILLIAM COWPER

One fact is clear: God did not separate himself
from human beings and their needs.
Nor did he limit his concern to the spiritual part
of man's personality.

ERWIN W. LUTZER

God's care will carry you so you can carry others.

ROBERT HAROLD SCHULLER

As a father has compassion for his children,
so the LORD has compassion for those who fear him.

PSALM 103:13 NRSV

Expectancy

*With God's power working in us, God can do much,
much more than anything we can ask or imagine.*

EPHESIANS 3:20 NCV

YOU'VE been waiting for months for the release of the sequel to your favorite movie. Finally, the time has come. You've waited in line, purchased your ticket, and found yourself a seat. You have an idea of what lies ahead, but you don't know exactly what's going to happen. All you know is that it's bound to be great.

That's the kind of expectation you can have about the life God has planned for you. He is more creative than any filmmaker, more amazing than any special effect, and more wonderful than any cinematic hero. You may not fully understand your story's beauty until you've reached the finale, but God promises every detail of the plot has been chosen for your ultimate good.

~~~~~~~~~~~~~~~~~~~~~~~~~~~~

The quality of our expectations determines
the quality of our actions.

ANDRÉ GODIN

There is something new every day
if you look for it.

HANNAH HURNARD

High expectations are the key to everything.

SAM WALTON

We block Christ's advance in our lives
by failure of expectation.

WILLIAM TEMPLE

God began doing a good work in you.
And he will continue it until it is finished
when Jesus Christ comes again.

PHILIPPIANS 1:6 NCV

Friendship

As iron sharpens iron, a friend sharpens a friend.
PROVERBS 27:17 NLT

GRADUATION is a time of change, excitement, expectation—and good-byes. A lot of the people you've grown close to over the past several years may not be headed the same direction God's leading you. But that doesn't mean your friendships can't continue to grow.

Keeping in touch across the miles takes effort. However, an e-mail, a crazy card, or a heartfelt phone call is all a friendship needs to spark many happy reunions. The friends God brings into your life are worth holding on to—and praying for. That includes the ones you haven't met yet. Along with those good-byes, you're also going to be saying a lot of glad-to-meet-yous. So open your heart. Some of your very best friends are waiting to meet you.

~~~~~~~~~~~~~~~~~~~~~~~~~~~~~~~

Friendship doesn't make you wealthy, but
true friendship will reveal the wealth within you.
AUTHOR UNKNOWN

Friendship is the inexpressible comfort of feeling safe with a person, having neither to weigh thoughts nor measure words.

GEORGE ELIOT

A true friend unbosoms freely, advises justly, assists readily, adventures boldly, takes all patiently, defends courageously, and continues a friend unchangeably.

WILLIAM PENN

Friendship is one of the sweetest joys of life. Many might have failed beneath the bitterness of their trial had they not found a friend.

CHARLES HADDON SPURGEON

Jesus said, "Greater love has no one than this, than to lay down one's life for his friends."

JOHN 15:13 NKJV

Purity

Let us purify ourselves from everything that contaminates body and spirit, perfecting holiness out of reverence for God.

2 CORINTHIANS 7:1 NIV

PICTURE Jesus as your constant companion, accompanying you for coffee with your friends, watching a DVD with you late into the night, cheering alongside you in the bleachers at a sporting event, or dropping by a convenience store with you to pick up a magazine. Does knowing Jesus is right beside you influence the choices you make or the language you use?

If there is any part of your life you'd be embarrassed for Jesus to see or hear, your purity may be in jeopardy. It's easy to forget God grieves when you go along with the crowd or your own less-than-pure desires or you do something you know you shouldn't. Dare to do what's right. Choose to keep your heart, and life, pure.

~~~~~~~~~~~~~~~~~~~~~~~~~~~~~

How to be pure? By steadfast longing for the one good, that is, God.

MEISTER ECKHART

There cannot be perfect transformation
without perfect pureness.

JOHN OF THE CROSS

Simplicity reaches out after God;
purity discovers and enjoys him.

THOMAS À KEMPIS

The insight that relates us to God arises
from purity of heart.

OSWALD CHAMBERS

Keep yourself pure.

1 TIMOTHY 5:22 NIV

Help

God is our shelter and strength,
always ready to help in times of trouble.

PSALM 46:1 GNT

HELP! A simple one-word prayer is often the most heartfelt. But, brevity doesn't bother God. He knows exactly what's behind your desperate plea. He also knows exactly what you need—and it may differ considerably from what you want. You may want circumstances to change immediately, even time to reverse itself.

Though God can, and does, work miracles, usually His help comes in subtler ways—through a renewal of strength, an outpouring of hope, or a peace that passes understanding. It may come through the words of a friend, the kindness of a stranger, or the awesome wonder of a thunderstorm. The help God offers varies from situation to situation. But one thing that never varies is God's dependability in answering your heartfelt prayer.

~~~~~~~~~~~~~~~~~~~~~~~~~~~~~

What other help could we ever need
than that of the Holy Spirit of God?

ANDREA GARNEY

Call the Comforter by the term you think best—
Advocate, Helper, Paraclete, the word conveys
the indefinable blessedness of his sympathy.

OSWALD CHAMBERS

Jesus promised his followers that
"The Strengthener" would be with them.
This promise is no lullaby for the fainthearted.
It is a blood transfusion for courageous living.

E. PAUL HOVEY

The Holy Spirit has promised to lead us
step by step into the fullness of truth.

LEON JOSEPH SUENENS

We can feel sure and say, "I will not be afraid
because the Lord is my helper."

HEBREWS 13:6 NCV

Finances

*Jesus said, "Real life is not measured
by how much we own."*

LUKE 12:15 NLT

A S THE proud owner of a diploma, the promise of financial freedom lies ahead. Budgets, taxes, and bottom lines will be more a part of your life than ever before. The challenge is to prevent what you own from owning you.

A rich life is not measured in paychecks or possessions. It's measured by the depth of your relationship with God and others. Handling money wisely by spending within your budget, using credit cautiously, saving for the future, and giving generously as God's Word directs, will help you keep money in perspective. It's just a tool, not a true treasure. Ask God to help you spend what you have, no matter how much or little that is, in a way that honors Him.

~~~~~~~~~~~~~~~~~~~~~~~~~~~~~

If a person gets his attitude toward money straight,
it will help straighten out almost every
other area in his life.

BILLY GRAHAM

Money has never yet made anyone rich.

SENECA

There is no portion of money that is our money,
and the rest God's money. It is all his;
he made it all, gives it all, and he has
simply trusted it to us for his service.

ADOLPHE MONOD

Use everything as if it belongs to God.
It does. You are his steward.

AUTHOR UNKNOWN

*Jesus said to them, "Take care! Be on your guard
against all kinds of greed; for one's life does not
consist in the abundance of possessions."*

LUKE 12:5 NRSV

Fresh Start

Count yourself lucky, how happy you must be—
you get a fresh start, your slate's wiped clean.

PSALM 32:1 THE MESSAGE

T AKING part in your class's commencement feels like a grand finale to your academic career. But the word *commence* actually means "to begin." Graduation day is more than an end to student life. It's a brand-new beginning, a fresh start.

Graduation isn't the only fresh start you'll experience in life. God offers you a commencement ceremony every time you need a second chance. Whenever you blow it, make a poor choice, or even all-out rebel, God says, "Let's begin again." You don't have to don a mortarboard. All God asks is that you come to Him in honest repentance and ask His forgiveness. From that moment, the past truly is history. All is forgiven and your fresh start is ready to commence.

~~~~~~~~~~~~~~~~~~~~~~~~~~~~~

With each sunrise, we start anew.

AUTHOR UNKNOWN

If you have made mistakes, even serious ones,
there is always another chance for you.
What we call failure is not the falling down,
but the staying down.

MARY PICKFORD

I like sunrises, Mondays, and new seasons.
God seems to be saying,
"With me you can always start afresh."

ADA LUM

Each day is a new life. Seize it. Live it.

DAVID GUY POWERS

If anyone is in Christ, there is a new creation:
everything old has passed away;
see, everything has become new!

2 CORINTHIANS 5:17 NRSV

Blessings

We praise God, the Father of our Lord Jesus Christ,
who has blessed us with every spiritual blessing in
the heavenly realms because we belong to Christ.

EPHESIANS 1:3 NLT

WHEN you think about counting your blessings, your mind most likely turns to those you can see—a warm place to live, food in the fridge, friends and family to hold you close. But the blessings God showers on you every day go far beyond what you can touch with your hands.

God's blessings include miracles like the process of prayer, a future home in heaven, and God's ultimate gift of salvation. Although blessings like these are really more than the human mind can understand, they are also easily taken for granted. Take time right now to send God a heartfelt thank-you note, via prayer. Ask Him to help your gratitude grow by making you increasingly more aware of every blessing He brings your way.

~~~~~~~~~~~~~~~~~~~~~~~~~~~~~~~

Reflect upon your present blessings, of which every
man has many, not on your past misfortunes,
of which all men have some.

CHARLES DICKENS

The more we count the blessings we have,
the less we crave the luxuries we haven't.

WILLIAM ARTHUR WARD

God is more anxious to bestow his blessings
on us than we are to receive them.

SAINT AUGUSTINE OF HIPPO

The best things are nearest; breath in your
nostrils, light in your eyes, flowers at your feet,
duties at your hand, the path of God
just before you.

ROBERT LOUIS STEVENSON

The LORD bless you and keep you; the LORD make
his face to shine upon you, and be gracious to you;
the LORD lift up his countenance upon you,
and give you peace.

NUMBER 6:24–26 NRSV

Comfort

Let your constant love comfort me,
as you have promised me.

PSALM 119:76 GNT

EVERYONE weeps. Even if your tears are not visible to those around you, life on this imperfect earth is bound to break your heart now and then. But you have a Father who loves you deeply. He doesn't want your heart to remain in shattered pieces. Like a mother who runs to her child's side the moment she hears a pain-filled cry, God is near, offering tender comfort when you need it most.

When your heart is crying out for healing, cry out to God. He'll never put you down for being overly emotional or tell you to grow up. Instead, He'll go to the source of your heartbreak, soothing your soul with peace and perspective. Allow God to dry your tears with His love.

~~~~~~~~~~~~~~~~~~~~~~~~~~~~~~

God does not comfort us to make us comfortable,
but to make us comforters.

HENRY JOWETT

It will greatly comfort you if you can see
God's hand in both your losses and your crosses.

CHARLES HADDON SPURGEON

No affliction nor temptation, no guilt nor
power of sin, no wounded spirit nor terrified
conscience, should induce us to despair
of help and comfort from God!

THOMAS SCOTT

In Christ the heart of the Father is revealed,
the higher comfort there cannot be
than to rest in the Father's heart.

ANDREW MURRAY

Whenever I am anxious and worried,
you comfort me and make me glad.

PSALM 94:19 GNT

Hospitality

*Cheerfully share your home with those who need
a meal or a place to stay.*

1 PETER 4:9 NLT

You don't have to own a house to make someone feel at home. All you have to do is open your heart. That's what hospitality is all about. It has nothing to do with your gourmet cooking skills or opulent guest accommodations. Cheerfully sharing what you have—be it little or much—is the only rule.

So, relax. Welcome in friends both old and new. Ask lots of questions and listen thoughtfully to their answers. Don't try to impress visitors with your immaculate housekeeping or culinary expertise. Warm them with genuine care and affection. The more you see guests—even unexpected ones—as a blessing instead of an inconvenience, the more you'll enjoy the adventure of opening your home, and heart, to others.

~~~~~~~~~~~~~~~~~~~~~~~~~~~~~~~

When there is room in the heart, there is room in the house.

DANISH PROVERB

Hospitality is one form of worship.

JEWISH PROVERB

Hospitality is threefold: for one's family,
this is necessity; for strangers, this is courtesy;
for the poor, this is charity.

THOMAS FULLER

Who practices hospitality entertains
God himself.

AUTHOR UNKNOWN

Do not neglect to show hospitality to strangers,
for by this some have entertained angels
without knowing it.

HEBREWS 13:2 NASB

Success

In everything you do, put God first, and he will direct you and crown your efforts with success.

PROVERBS 3:6 TLB

PERSONAL success cannot be measured by the make of your car, the size of your paycheck, or even the recognition you receive for a job well done. True success depends on who you are, not on what you've accomplished.

God created you with a unique potential only you can fulfill. The more you focus on becoming who God intended you to be, the more successful you'll become—no matter what career path you choose.

Use the gifts God's given you to the best of your ability. Ask God to guide you in making wise decisions. Seek God's approval more than the approval of those around you. Then, your success is sure.

~~~~~~~~~~~~~~~~~~~~~~~~~~~~~~

What a tragedy to climb the ladder of success, only to discover that the ladder was leaning against the wrong wall.

<div align="right">ERWIN W. LUTZER</div>

It is not your business to succeed,
but to do right;
when you have done so,
the rest lies with God.

C. S. LEWIS

Success is a journey, not a destination.

BEN SWEETLAND

We should work to become, not to acquire.

AUTHOR UNKNOWN

O LORD, we beseech you, give us success!

PSALM 118:25 NRSV

Gentleness

Live a life worthy of the calling you have received.
Be completely humble and gentle.

EPHESIANS 4:1–2 NIV

REMEMBER wrestling on the floor when you were a kid? The inevitable parental warning usually went something like this: "Don't play rough or someone's going to get hurt!" That same warning holds true today. Anytime you interact with another person, there's a chance someone may get hurt. That's why being gentle with one another is so important.

It doesn't matter if you're a big, burly guy or a gal who's never met a risk she didn't want to take. Gentleness is not a personality trait. It's a character quality worth putting into practice.

Whomever you spend time with today, friends and strangers alike, play gently. Let your words, your tone of voice, your actions, and even your attitude reflect a tender, godly spirit.

~~~~~~~~~~~~~~~~~~~~~~~~~~~~

Power can do by gentleness what
violence fails to accomplish.

LATIN PROVERB

Nothing is so strong as gentleness,
nothing so gentle as real strength.

SAINT FRANCIS DE SALES

Feelings are everywhere ... be gentle.

J. MASAI

If you would reap praise, sow the seeds:
gentle words and useful deeds.

BENJAMIN FRANKLIN

Let your gentleness be known to everyone.

PHILIPPIANS 4:5 NRSV

Church

Since you are so eager to have spiritual gifts,
ask God for those that will be of real help
to the whole church.

1 CORINTHIANS 14:12 NLT

THERE'S a church out there that needs you. It isn't complete without you. What awaits is a support group of friends, opportunities to use the gifts God's given you, and an environment where you can grow. But you have to make the first move.

If graduation has taken you in a new direction, don't put off finding a church you can call home. If you're already part of a church, check your involvement level. If you're over- or under-involved, ask God to help you find a healthy balance. Then use your newfound graduate freedom to make a wise choice to follow His leading. Honor God and feed your own hungry soul by attending a weekly service. Go with a teachable mind, a servant's heart—and enjoy.

~~~~~~~~~~~~~~~~~~~~~~~~~~~~~~

Church attendance is as vital to a disciple as
a transfusion of rich, healthy blood to a sick man.

DWIGHT L. MOODY

The church is an organism, not an organization;
a movement, not a monument.

CHARLES COLSON

Church-goers are like coals in a fire.
When they cling together, they keep
the flame aglow; when they separate, they die out.

BILLY GRAHAM

A church is a hospital for sinners,
not a museum for saints.

L. L. NASH

*Jesus said, "I also say to you that you are Peter,
and upon this rock I will build My church;
and the gates of Hades will not overpower it."*

MATTHEW 16:18 NASB

Security

God's truth stands firm like a foundation stone
with this inscription:
"The Lord knows those who are his."

2 Timothy 2:19 NLT

There are not many things in life that can be considered totally secure and immovable. However, the ground is usually one of them. Yet, all it takes is a shifting fault line to remind you even the solid foundation beneath your feet is not fully trustworthy.

God has no fault lines. His promises, power, truth, and love are your only true security. When the world around you starts to shake, relationships shift, your health crumbles, or your finances threaten to fall off the deep end, remind yourself of Whom you're standing on for support. Rest the full weight of your troubles on the all-powerful God. He's a foundation that will never fail.

~~~~~~~~~~~~~~~~~~~~~~~~~~~~~~~

No matter what may be the test,
God will take care of you.

<div align="right">C. D. Martin</div>

In God's faithfulness lies eternal security.

CORRIE TEN BOOM

The saints in heaven are happier
but no more secure than are true believers
here in this world.

LORAINE BOETTNER

Security is not the absence of danger,
but the presence of God,
no matter what the danger.

AUTHOR UNKNOWN

They that trust in the LORD shall be as mount Zion,
which cannot be removed, but abideth forever.

PSALM 125:1 KJV

Speech

*Jesus said, "A good person produces
good words from a good heart."*

MATTHEW 12:35 NLT

YOU don't have to be a graduate to know an apple tree produces apples. You wouldn't expect it to produce watermelons or kumquats. It only produces fruit in keeping with the kind of tree it is.

Your heart is the same way. It produces words that reflect the "kind" of heart you have. Sure, people can fake it for a while. They can try to sound sweet and sincere when their hearts are really filled with anger or pride. But eventually that "natural" fruit is going to blossom.

Watching your words begins with examining your own heart. Ask God if you have any negative attitudes that need pruning. With His help, you can consistently give words of love, instead of carelessly tossing rotten verbal apples.

~~~~~~~~~~~~~~~~~~~~~~~~~~~~~~

Speaking without thinking is shooting
without aiming.

SIR WILLIAM GURNEY BENHAM

It is easier to look wise than to talk wisely.

SAINT AMBROSE

Kind words produce their image on men's souls,
and a beautiful image it is. They smooth,
and quiet, and comfort the hearer.

BLAISE PASCAL

Good words are worth much, and cost little.

GEORGE HERBERT

When you talk, do not say harmful things.
But say what people need—
words that will help others become stronger.

EPHESIANS 4:29 NCV

Nature

God looked over all that he had made,
and it was excellent in every way.

GENESIS 1:31 TLB

TO BETTER understand the heart of an artist, you need to study his work. Examine his brush strokes. Note his favorite color palette. Consider his subject matter. Sit and enjoy the beauty of his creation.

God is the ultimate Artist. His creations are so amazing that a lifetime is not long enough to fully appreciate them. However, you can understand God's heart a little better by studying His work. Even the simplest flower shows His creativity, attention to detail, organizational skills, and love of beauty.

Wherever you are right now, take a quick peek outside. What does what you see teach you about the God you cannot see? Take a moment to tell God what you think about His handiwork.

~~~~~~~~~~~~~~~~~~~~~~~~~~~~~

The more I study nature,
the more I am amazed at the Creator.

LOUIS PASTEUR

Nature is but a name for an effect
whose cause is God.

WILLIAM COWPER

I love to think of nature as an unlimited
broadcasting station through which God speaks
to us every hour, if we will only tune in.

GEORGE WASHINGTON CARVER

We can almost smell the aroma of God's beauty
in the fresh spring flowers. His breath surrounds us
in the warm summer breezes.

GALE HEIDE

The heavens declare the glory of God;
and the firmament sheweth his handiwork.

PSALM 19:1 KJV

Joy

I will rejoice in the LORD,
I will be joyful in God my Savior.

HABAKKUK 3:18 NIV

WHEN a baby sees his mother's face, every part of his body wiggles, jiggles, and smiles with delight. His source of joy is the one he loves, the one he recognizes—even at an early age—the one who loves him in return.

Growing in your relationship with God is not just an exercise in getting to know the Bible better. It is all about getting to know God better, up close and personal. He wants to be the source of your joy and delight.

Even when circumstances are anything but happy, true joy is as close as God's loving presence. Spend time talking to Him, finding comfort in His promises and contentment in His love. There is no deeper joy this side of heaven.

~~~~~~~~~~~~~~~~~~~~~~~~~~~~

Life need not be easy to be joyful. Joy is not the absence of trouble but the presence of Christ.

WILLIAM VAN DER HOVEN

Happiness depends on what happens;
joy does not.

OSWALD CHAMBERS

Joy is the most infallible sign of
the presence of God.

LEON BLOY

Joy is an unceasing fountain bubbling up in
the heart; a secret spring the world can't see
and doesn't know anything about.

DWIGHT L. MOODY

Jesus said, "Ask and you will receive.
And your joy will be the fullest joy."

JOHN 16:24 NCV

Health

I am the LORD, who heals you.

EXODUS 15:26 NIV

YOUR body is an incredible gift, but it's not an indestructible one. Bodies break down, wear out, and catch all kinds of diseases. Even if you take good care of yourself—eat a balanced diet, get enough sleep, exercise regularly—your body may not always run smoothly.

When your health goes downhill, get God involved. He doesn't discourage you from seeking medical treatment. He simply encourages you to turn to Him as part of the healing process. God wants you to be healthy and whole in every area of your life—body, soul and spirit. Trust Him to help you reach healing in the way He knows is best.

~~~~~~~~~~~~~~~~~~~~~~~~~~~~

Take care of your health,
that it may serve you to serve God.

SAINT FRANCIS DE SALES

The part can never be well unless
the whole is well.

PLATO

To be "whole" is to be spiritually, emotionally,
and physically healthy.
Jesus lived in perfect wholeness.

COLIN URQUHART

Our prayers should be for a sound mind
in a healthy body.

JUVENAL

*I wish above all things that thou mayest prosper
and be in health, even as thy soul prospereth.*

3 JOHN 2 KJV

Scripture

Guard my words as your most precious possession.
PROVERBS 7:2 TLB

THE Bible isn't homework. It's not a textbook you have to study or an assignment you need to complete. It's a love letter from Someone who cherishes having a relationship with you that will never end.

So read the Bible like you do a letter from a close friend. Don't hurry through it. Savor it. See if your Friend has any requests you need to fulfill or advice for you to follow. See if what's said reveals anything new about how your Friend views you, others, or world situations. Then, respond with a love note of your own, written in the words of a heartfelt prayer.

~~~~~~~~~~~~~~~~~~~~~~~~~~~~~

When you read God's word you must
constantly be saying to yourself,
"It is talking to me, and about me."
SØREN KIERKEGAARD

God did not write a book and send it by messenger to be read at a distance by unaided minds. He spoke a Book and lives in His spoken words, constantly speaking His words and causing the power of them to persist across the years.

A. W. TOZER

The Bible is God's chart for you to steer by, to keep you from the bottom of the sea, and to show you where the harbor is, and how to reach it without running on rocks and bars.

HENRY WARD BEECHER

When you have read the Bible, you will know it is the word of God, because you will have found it the key to your own heart, your own happiness and your duty.

WOODROW WILSON

Using the Scriptures, the person who serves
God will be ready and will have everything
he needs to do every good work.

2 TIMOTHY 3:17 NCV

Forgiveness

Forgive each other just as God forgave you in Christ.
EPHESIANS 4:32 NCV

A GRUDGE is a heavy weight to carry. It can consume your thoughts, infect your attitude, and even adversely affect your health. You can't get rid of it by simply trying to forget you've been hurt. You have to replace it with something that heals the pain. That "something" is forgiveness.

Forgiving someone doesn't excuse what happened or automatically mend a relationship. It doesn't mean you're "weak" for giving in. It means you're strong enough to willingly choose to imitate God's character. It means you're courageous enough to practice real love in an often unloving world.

This is something that requires God's help. If there's a grudge currently weighing on you, go to God. Ask Him to help you honestly forgive—and let the healing begin.

~~~~~~~~~~~~~~~~~~~~~~~~~~~~~

Forgiveness means letting go of the past.
GERALD JAMPOLSKY

When you forgive, you in no way change
the past—but you sure do change the future.

BERNARD MELTZER

Forgiveness is the key that unlocks the door of
resentment and the handcuffs of hate.
It is a power that breaks the chains of bitterness
and the shackles of selfishness.

CORRIE TEN BOOM

Forgiveness is God's command.

MARTIN LUTHER

Be gentle and ready to forgive; never hold grudges.
Remember, the Lord forgave you,
so you must forgive others.

COLOSSIANS 3:13 TLB

Perseverance

Let us run the race before us and never give up.
HEBREWS 12:1 NCV

IN TRACK and field, there are a few common-sense tips to winning a race: stay in shape, stay alert, pace yourself, keep your eyes on the goal, and never give up.

Life can feel like a very long race at times. It's easy to get tired or discouraged when obstacles get in your way, when it feels as though the people running next to you would rather see you fail than succeed. But God has a race that's set just for you. It's not a saunter through the park. It's a race that will push you to your full potential. But keep moving. God's cheering you on every step of the way.

~~~~~~~~~~~~~~~~~~~~~~~~~~~~~~

Permanence, perseverance, and persistence in spite of all obstacles, discouragements, and impossibilities—it is this that in all things distinguishes the strong soul from the weak.
SIR FRANCIS DRAKE

There must be a beginning to any great matter,
but the continuing to the end until it be
thoroughly finished yields the true glory.

THOMAS CARLYLE

Energy and persistence conquer all things.

BENJAMIN FRANKLIN

Great works are performed, not by strength,
but by perseverance.

SAMUEL JOHNSON

You must hold on, so you can do what God wants
and receive what he has promised.

HEBREWS 10:36 NCV

Goodness

Ask where the good way is, and walk in it.

JEREMIAH 6:16 NIV

GOOD seems so relative. Ice cream is good. So are the Broncos. You can have a good attitude, good penmanship, or get a good deal on a used car. Some people even preach, "If it feels good, do it!"

The best way to know what is truly good is to remove an *o* from the word itself. All that remains is *God*. Whatever God would do, say, or praise in any given situation is what is wholly good.

Being a genuinely good person means being a godly person: someone whose heart and actions make God smile. Make that your measure of having a *good* day.

~~~~~~~~~~~~~~~~~~~~~~~~~~~~~~

Think of how good God is! He gives us
the physical, mental, and spiritual ability
to work in his kingdom,
and then he rewards us for doing it!

ERWIN W. LUTZER

God's goodness is the root of all goodness;
and our goodness, if we have any,
springs out of his goodness

WILLIAM TYNDALE

God is all that is good, in my sight,
and the goodness that everything has is his.

JULIAN OF NORWICH

The goodness of God knows how to use
our disordered wishes and actions, often lovingly
turning them to our advantage while always
preserving the beauty of his order.

SAINT BERNARD OF CLAIRVAUX

O taste and see that the LORD is good;
happy are those who take refuge in him.

PSALM 34:8 NRSV

Prayer

Never stop praying.

1 Thessalonians 5:17 CEV

YOU don't need words to talk to God. Tears, sighs, and even silence can communicate with your Heavenly Father in the same way that a look on your face can communicate what you're feeling to a friend. Those who know you well can understand what runs even deeper than words, just by being in your presence.

The Creator of the universe is always in your presence—although that's easy to forget at times. Even though He knows your every thought, prayer reminds you God is near. It prompts you to include Him in every aspect of your day, in even the little details.

When you wake up, before you fall asleep, whether you're feeling fearful or joyful ... anytime is the right time to talk to God.

~~~~~~~~~~~~~~~~~~~~~~~~~~~~~

Let your first "Good morning"
be to your Father in heaven.

Karl G. Maeser

We should speak to God from our own hearts
and talk to him as a child talks to his father.

CHARLES HADDON SPURGEON

All who call on God in true faith, earnestly from
the heart, will certainly be heard and will receive
what they have asked and desired.

MARTIN LUTHER

When you can't put your prayers into words,
God hears your heart.

AUTHOR UNKNOWN

God listens to us every time we ask him.
So we know that he gives us the things
that we ask from him.

1 JOHN 5:15 NCV

Work

*A faithful employee is as refreshing
as a cool day in the hot summertime.*

PROVERBS 25:13 TLB

WHEN you look back at the years of schoolwork you have behind you, you can feel proud about everything you've achieved. But there's so much more for you to accomplish. Don't let the thought of all the work that's ahead discourage you. Let it inspire you. Work is more than something you do to pay the bills. It's a way of making a positive impact on the world around you and reflecting God's example of excellence. It's an opportunity to use the unique combination of gifts and talents God has given you.

It doesn't matter whether you work on Wall Street or at a drive-through window. Put your whole heart into whatever you do. God can use your efforts to do great things.

~~~~~~~~~~~~~~~~~~~~~~~~~~~~~

He who labors diligently need never despair, for all things are accomplished by diligence and labor.

MENANDER

There's no labor a man can do that's undignified,
if he does it right.

BILL COSBY

Honest labor bears a lovely face.

THOMAS DEKKER

Work is not a curse, it is a blessing from God.

JOHN PAUL II

Whatever your task, put yourselves into it,
as done for the Lord and not for your masters.

COLOSSIANS 3:23 NRSV

Grace

*How rich is God's grace, which he has given
to us so fully and freely.*

EPHESIANS 1:7–8 NCV

GRACE is the ultimate free gift. You don't deserve it. You can't earn it. It will never wear out or grow thin. It fits you perfectly, no matter who you are. All you have to do to receive this life-changing gift is ask for it.

The gift of grace is free, but that doesn't mean it didn't come at a high price. God asked Jesus to give His life so grace could change not only your destiny here on Earth but also for eternity. He believed you were worth it.

Take a moment to think about God's gift of grace—and what it cost to extend it so freely to you. Thank God for the difference it's made in your life.

~~~~~~~~~~~~~~~~~~~~~~~~~~~~

There is nothing but God's grace.
We walk upon it; we breathe it;
we live and die by it;
it makes the nails and axles of the universe.

ROBERT LOUIS STEVENSON

Grace is love that cares and stoops and rescues.

JOHN STOTT

Grace is always given to those ready
to give thanks for it.

THOMAS À KEMPIS

A state of mind that sees God in everything
is evidence of growth in grace
and a thankful heart.

CHARLES FINNEY

Grace to you and peace from God our Father,
and the Lord Jesus Christ.

ROMANS 1:7 KJV

Encouragement

*Think of ways to encourage one another
to outbursts of love and good deeds.*

HEBREWS 10:24 NLT

ENCOURAGEMENT is more than building others up with your words. It's helping them find the courage to move ahead in a positive direction.

When God opens your eyes to someone who's discouraged, disappointed, or in need of comfort, ask Him for the wisdom to know the best words and actions to share. Let God's love for you encourage your own heart so you can reach out in confidence, kindness, and humility.

Whatever you do or say, remember it's God's love and power working through you that ultimately help another person—not your own superior counseling abilities. When God uses you in the lives of others, always thank Him for the privilege of being an encourager.

~~~~~~~~~~~~~~~~~~~~~~~~~~~~~

Encouragement is oxygen to the soul.

GEORGE M. ADAMS

One of the highest of human duties
is the duty of encouragement.

WILLIAM BARCLAY

Encouragement costs you nothing to give,
but it is priceless to receive.

AUTHOR UNKNOWN

More people fail for lack of encouragement
than for any other reason.

AUTHOR UNKNOWN

Patience and encouragement come from God.

ROMANS 15:5 NCV

Family

If you honor your father and mother,
"you will live a long life, full of blessing."
EPHESIANS 6:3 NLT

FOR many students, graduation marks the time when life at home draws to a close. The change from living with your folks to being on your own is an exciting one. But your address isn't the only thing that undergoes a transition. So does your relationship with your family. As always, God provides guidelines on handling the relational challenges ahead.

No matter what your age, God asks you honor your parents. Period. He doesn't add "if they deserve it" or "until you graduate." Honor is to be a lifelong gift from you to your parents.

No matter what your family background, God can guide you through every season of your life in a way that honors the parents God gave you.

~~~~~~~~~~~~~~~~~~~~~~~~~~~~~~

The family is the most basic unit of government.
As the first community to which a person
is attached and the first authority under which
a person learns to live, the family establishes
society's most basic values.

CHARLES W. COLSON

A family is a place where principles are hammered and honed on the anvil of everyday living.

CHARLES R. SWINDOLL

Loving relationships are a family's best protection against the challenges of the world.

BERNIE WIEBE

The family is an everlasting anchorage, a quiet harbor.

RICHARD BYRD

*I bow my knees before the Father,
from whom every family in heaven
and on earth takes its name.*

EPHESIANS 3:14–15 NRSV

Confidence

You have been my hope, O Sovereign LORD,
my confidence since my youth.

PSALM 71:5 NIV

THE first rule of any job interview is to act confident. But, where does that confidence come from? Is it found in your education? Your natural abilities? Your family connections? The new designer suit you happen to be wearing?

Confidence in anything other than God's love for you and His power working through you is not sturdy enough on which to build an accurate self-image. Self-assurance is great, but God-assurance is what's going to keep you going through the ups and downs of life.

When you're faced with a challenge, thank God for the strengths and assets He's provided you. Then refuse to rely solely on them. Firmly place your confidence on God—who He is and who He says you are in Him.

~~~~~~~~~~~~~~~~~~~~~~~~~~~~~

I place no hope in my strength, nor in my works:
but all my confidence is in God.

FRANÇOIS RABELAIS

Our confidence in Christ ... awakens us,
urges us on, and makes us active in living
righteous lives and doing good.
There is no self-confidence to compare with this.

ULRICH ZWINGLI

Above all things, never think that you're not
good enough yourself. My belief is that in life
people will take you at your own reckoning.

ANTHONY TROLLOPE

Nothing can be done without
hope and confidence.

HELEN KELLER

The LORD will be your confidence
and will keep your foot from being snared.

PROVERBS 3:26 NIV

Generosity

Those who are generous are blessed,
for they share their bread with the poor.

PROVERBS 22:9 NRSV

PICTURE a miser. Someone like Ebenezer Scrooge will do. He holds on tightly to everything he owns. He's focused on his own needs, the value of his possessions, what he hopes to attain—never on the needs of others. The struggles of those around him do nothing to move his heart. That's because his heart is totally wrapped up in himself.

Now picture a person whose life is exactly the opposite. That's generosity in action: holding on to money and possessions loosely; recognizing that everything one has is a gift; making it easy to share those gifts with others; being other-centered, instead of self-centered.

While being miserly leads to misery; generosity leads to true wealth—the joy of a life rich in relationship, community, and contentment.

~~~~~~~~~~~~~~~~~~~~~~~~~~~~~~

He who gives what he would as readily
throw away, gives without generosity;
for the essence of generosity is in self-sacrifice.

SIR HENRY TAYLOR

The truly generous is the truly wise,
and he who loves not others, lives unblest.

HENRY HOME

You do not have to be rich to be generous.
If he has the spirit of true generosity,
a pauper can give like a prince.

CORRINE U. WELLS

The test of generosity is not how much you give,
but how much you have left.

AUTHOR UNKNOWN

A generous person will be enriched.

PROVERBS 11:25 NRSV

Trust

WHAT do you do when your heart is tugging you one way, but you know God is telling you to go in exactly the opposite direction? Trust God. The guidelines He has given you in the Bible do not change, no matter what the circumstances. What He says is always true, always right, always wise.

Your heart, however well-intentioned, can be swayed by emotion, public opinion, even by things like exhaustion or pride. It's not a trustworthy compass when it comes to leading you in the right direction.

When a decision comes down to following your heart or following God, you don't need to ask for directions. There's only one right way to go.

~~~~~~~~~~~~~~~~~~~~~~~~~~~~~

All I have seen teaches me to trust
the Creator for all I have not seen.

RALPH WALDO EMERSON

I have held many things in my hands,
and I have lost them all; but whatever
I have placed in God's hands, that I still possess.

CORRIE TEN BOOM

Trust the past to God's mercy, the present to
God's love and the future to God's providence.

SAINT AUGUSTINE OF HIPPO

Trust in God and you are never to be
confounded in time or in eternity.

DWIGHT L. MOODY

Trust in Him at all times, O people;
pour out your heart before him;
God is a refuge for us.

PSALM 62:8 NRSV

Acceptance

Honor God by accepting each other,
as Christ has accepted you.

Romans 15:7 CEV

GOD accepts you—warts and all. Can you do the same for those around you? It's easy to get off track. A different race, different religious beliefs, even a different style of clothes can lead you to make judgments before you even carry on a conversation with someone.

The key is to bypass what you see and focus on what you know. God created each person with great love and care. God accepts each person, even if he or she has not accepted Him. The more you learn to view others through God's love, instead of sizing them up with your eyes, the easier it will be to accept them as equals, treat them as friends, and love them as God's precious children.

~~~~~~~~~~~~~~~~~~~~~~~~~~~~~

If God accepts me as I am,
then I had better do the same.

HUGH MONTEFIORE

Just as I am, thou wilt receive, will welcome,
pardon, cleanse, relieve; because
thy promise I believe, O Lamb of God, I come.

CHARLOTTE ELLIOTT

Jesus accepts you the way you are,
but loves you too much to leave you that way.

LEE VENDEN

Accept the fact that you are accepted.

PAUL TILLICH

To the praise of the glory of his grace,
wherein he hath made us accepted in the beloved.

EPHESIANS 1:6 KJV

Courage

The Lord is my light and my salvation—
so why should I be afraid?

Psalm 27:1 NLT

IT TAKES courage to go where God leads. He'll often take you right to the doorstep of your greatest fears, put you face-to-face with someone you can't stand to be around, or bring a situation into your life that seems impossible to work out. Don't panic. Those are the times when you can really see God's power in action.

You were never created to handle tough times alone. Consider David. The only reason he could conquer a giant was because God was with him. You have the same advantage. God is fighting every battle with you, never against you.

So, take courage. Stand up to the giants in your life. With God's help, victory is at hand.

~~~~~~~~~~~~~~~~~~~~~~~~~~~~

Courage is fear that has said its prayers.

<div align="right">

Dorothy Bernard

</div>

Courage faces fear and thereby masters it.

MARTIN LUTHER KING JR.

Fear can keep a man out of danger,
but courage can support him in it.

THOMAS FULLER

Courage consists not in blindly overlooking
danger, but in seeing and conquering it!

JEAN PAUL RICHTER

Be strong and of good courage; do not be afraid,
nor be dismayed, for the LORD your God
is with you wherever you go.

JOSHUA 1:9

Thoughts

*Let God transform you into a new person
by changing the way you think.*

ROMANS 12:2 NLT

EVERY action, attitude, and plan for the future begins in one place: your mind. That's why God cares so much about what's going on in your cranium. What you spend time thinking about determines what you will spend time doing—and ultimately who you will become.

Before you knew God, your thoughts pretty much centered around one thing: you—meeting your own needs, keeping yourself happy. But times have changed. So should your thoughts.

Notice where you let your mind wander. If it heads down any road you feel God would prefer you not to go, consciously change directions. If certain activities negatively influence your thoughts, find alternative ways to spend your time. Changing your mind really can change your life.

~~~~~~~~~~~~~~~~~~~~~~~~~~~~~~

Our best friends and our worst enemies are
our thoughts. A thought can do us more good
than a doctor or a banker or a faithful friend.
It can also do us more harm than a brick.

FRANK CRANE

Keep your thoughts right, for as you think,
so are you.

HENRY H. BUCKLEY

It concerns us to keep a strict guard upon
our thoughts, because God takes
particular notice of them.

MATTHEW HENRY

Think positively and masterfully, with confidence
and faith, and life becomes more secure,
more fraught with action,
richer in achievement and experience.

EDDIE RICKENBACKER

Keep your minds on whatever is true, pure, right,
holy, friendly, and proper. Don't ever stop thinking
about what is truly worthwhile and worthy of praise.

PHILIPPIANS 4:8 CEV

Humility

With humility comes wisdom.

PROVERBS 11:2 NLT

UNLIKE what you see in the movies, humility is a good thing. It isn't putting yourself down or trying to blend in with the wallpaper. Humility is simply seeing yourself from God's point of view. It's accepting that you're worth no more, or less, than any other person whom God dearly loves.

Once you have a clear view of yourself, you can get a clearer view of what God wants you to do. You won't argue over what you think is too hard for you to tackle or way beneath your dignity. You can do whatever God asks—and rest in knowing that with God, your best is always good enough.

~~~~~~~~~~~~~~~~~~~~~~~~~~~~~

Humility is nothing else but a true knowledge and awareness of oneself as one really is.

THE CLOUD OF UNKNOWING

For those who would learn God's ways,
humility is the first thing, humility is the second,
humility is the third.

SAINT AUGUSTINE OF HIPPO

If you are humble, nothing will touch you,
neither praise nor disgrace,
because you know what you are.

MOTHER TERESA

It is no great thing to be humble when you
are brought low; but to be humble when
you are praised is a great and rare attainment.

SAINT BERNARD OF CLAIRVAUX

Be clothed with humility, for "God resists the proud,
but gives grace to the humble."

1 PETER 5:5

Love

WANT to know what love looks like? Look at God. Consider His sacrifice, His patience, His comfort, His faithfulness, His generosity. God's creativity in expressing love is so great, it's almost incomprehensible.

Consider how your love stands up next to His. Don't get discouraged. You're not God. At times, your love still falters and fails. But God's love is at work in your life. He's helping you love others in the same wonderful way He so deeply loves you.

Let God's creative compassion inspire you to love others well. Ask for His help in knowing the best way to express your love so it meets needs, builds relationships, and warms hearts. Then, take a moment to sit back and enjoy His love for you.

~~~~~~~~~~~~~~~~~~~~~~~~~~~~~~~

Love seeks one thing only:
the good of the one loved.

THOMAS MERTON

He who is filled with love is filled
with God himself.

SAINT AUGUSTINE OF HIPPO

I have found the paradox that if I love
until it hurts, then there is no hurt,
but only more love.

MOTHER TERESA

Love is the only spiritual power that can
overcome the self-centeredness
that is inherent in being alive.

ARNOLD JOSEPH TOYNBEE

Beloved, let us love one another, for love is from God;
and everyone who loves is born of God
and knows God.

1 JOHN 4:7 NASB

Rest

Jesus said, "Come to me, all of you who are weary and carry heavy burdens, and I will give you rest."
MATTHEW 11:28 NLT

REMEMBER that heavy backpack you lugged around all through school? Imagine carrying not only your own books, but the books of your entire senior class. Impossible? You bet. Your backpack—as well as your back—was not designed to carry that kind of a load.

When life starts weighing on you like an overstuffed backpack, chances are you may be carrying more than God intended for you. Take the load to God. Lay it out before Him. Ask Him what to pick back up and what to leave behind. Lean on Him for strength with any especially heavy problems.

Then, rest against God's strong arms. Close your eyes for just a few minutes and enjoy a mini-retreat. God's presence can lighten the heaviest heart.

~~~~~~~~~~~~~~~~~~~~~~~~~~~~~

Life lived amidst tension and busyness needs leisure—leisure that re-creates and renews.
NEIL C. STRAIT

Take rest; a field that has rested gives
a bountiful crop.

OVID

Jesus knows we must come apart and rest a while,
or else we may just plain come apart.

VANCE HAVNER

How beautiful it is to do nothing,
and then rest afterward.

SPANISH PROVERB

He said, "My presence shall go with you,
and I will give you rest."

EXODUS 33:14 NASB

Integrity

The integrity of the upright guides them.

PROVERBS 11:3 NRSV

WHEN storms begin to blow, the integrity of a building is revealed—the strength of its foundation, the practicality of its design, and the quality of its building materials. Will it stand or will it fall?

The same holds true for your own integrity. When the pressure is on, weak spots in your faith or character readily come to light. If this happens, take note. Your integrity matures over time. If you've made choices that weren't sound in the past, make better choices today. Make sure your foundation rests solely on what God says is true, not on what your emotions or contemporary culture says is right and fair.

Then, turn your face toward the wind with confidence. You and your integrity are built to last.

~~~~~~~~~~~~~~~~~~~~~~~~~~~~~

Integrity is the first step to true greatness.

CHARLES SIMMONS

There is no such thing as a minor lapse
of integrity.

TOM PETERS

Integrity is not a conditional word.
It doesn't blow in the wind or change with
the weather. It is your inner image of yourself,
and if you look in there and see a man
who won't cheat, then you know he never will.

JOHN D. MACDONALD

Integrity is the noblest possession.

LATIN PROVERB

We take thought beforehand and aim to be honest
and absolutely above suspicion, not only in the sight
of the Lord but also in the sight of men.

2 CORINTHIANS 8:21 AMP

Time

These are evil times, so make every minute count.
EPHESIANS 5:16 CEV

You only get one "today." After 1440 minutes, your today becomes a yesterday. No do-overs, no second chances, no turning back the clock. Choosing how you'll spend the time you have is a big responsibility. You can waste it on what is worthless or invest it in what will last throughout eternity. The choice is yours.

God wants you to live life to the fullest. That begins with making wise, premeditated choices about how you'll spend the days ahead. It doesn't mean you need to book every minute on your calendar or that lying on the beach soaking up a little sun is a waste of time. Just be aware of how easily time slips away—and spend it wisely in light of your priorities.

~~~~~~~~~~~~~~~~~~~~~~~~~~~~

Time is not a commodity that can be stored for future use. It must be invested hour by hour.
<div align="right">THOMAS EDISON</div>

Time is given us to use in view of eternity.
AUTHOR UNKNOWN

What is time? Months, years, centuries—
these are but arbitrary and outward signs,
the measure of time, not time itself.
Time is the Life of the soul.
HENRY WADSWORTH LONGFELLOW

Only eternal values can give meaning
to temporal ones.
Time must be the servant of eternity.
ERWIN W. LUTZER

*To every thing there is a season,
and a time to every purpose under the heaven.*
ECCLESIASTES 3:1 KJV

Belief

Jesus said, "Anything is possible if a person believes."
MARK 9:23 NLT

As a KID, you probably believed some unbelievable things, like the tooth fairy exchanged molars for cash or Santa shimmied down your chimney on Christmas Eve. What you believed, true or not, influenced your actions. You put your tooth under your pillow and left cookies out for Santa.

Some aspects of God seem unbelievable. But He's no fairy tale. Put the historicity of Jesus and the faithfulness of God's promises to the test. Know what you believe and why.

Then, don't just say you believe in God; act on that belief. Release guilt and regret, believing God's forgiven you. Risk being authentically you, believing God created you for a unique purpose. Reach out to others, believing love is God's highest aim for your life.

~~~~~~~~~~~~~~~~~~~~~~~~~~~~~~

We can believe what we choose.
We are answerable for what we choose to believe.
JOHN HENRY NEWMAN

If easy belief is impossible, it is that we may learn
what belief is and in whom it is to be placed.

F. D. MAURICE

I now believe that the balance of reasoned
considerations tells heavily in
favor of the religious,
even of the Christian view of the world.

C. E. M. JOAD

The point of having an open mind,
like having an open mouth,
is to close it on something solid.

G. K. CHESTERTON

We believe with our hearts,
and so we are made right with God.

ROMANS 10:10 NCV

Satisfaction

[The LORD] satisfies your desires with good things.
PSALM 103:5 NIV

THINK about the feeling of satisfaction you get when you've eaten a good meal of your favorite foods and you wisely choose to stop eating before you go from full to stuffed.

That's how God wants you to feel about life. A job well done, a dream fulfilled, a relationship healed, a confidence in knowing how much God loves you. There are numerous things God can bring your way that satisfy your heart.

God knows every one of your deepest desires. Trying to fill these desires on your own can lead to frustration—or even lead you away from God. But, letting God fill your desires in His way and in His time leads to satisfaction that lasts.

~~~~~~~~~~~~~~~~~~~~~~~~~~~~~

People who wait around for life to supply their satisfaction usually find boredom instead.
WILLIAM MENNINGER

The world without Christ will not
satisfy the soul.

THOMAS BROOKS

Do not give your heart to that which
does not satisfy your heart.

ABBA POEMEN

Look at a day when you are supremely satisfied
at the end. It's not a day when you lounged
around doing nothing. It's when you've
had everything to do, and you've done it.

MARGARET THATCHER

That everyone may eat and drink,
and find satisfaction in all his toil—
this is the gift of God.

ECCLESIASTES 3:13 NIV

God's Faithfulness

A faithful God who does no wrong,
upright and just is he.

DEUTERONOMY 32:4 NIV

*N*EVER is a tricky word to use properly. It means no exceptions, no chance, no way—ever. But with God, *never* is both accurate and encouraging. God never changes. His promises never fail. His patience never falters. His power never diminishes. His love never ends.

All of these things that will never happen with God are the result of His faithfulness. God is as good as His Word. That means you can count on God, even if others have let you down.

Give God the chance to demonstrate His faithfulness to you. Be bold in following through on what you believe He wants you to do. Then, thank Him for the variety of ways He comes through for you.

~~~~~~~~~~~~~~~~~~~~~~~~~~~~~~

In God's faithfulness lies eternal security.

CORRIE TEN BOOM

What more powerful consideration can be
thought on to make us true to God,
than the faithfulness and truth of God to us?

WILLIAM GURNALL

God is faithful, and if we serve him faithfully,
he will provide for our needs.

SAINT RICHARD OF CHICHESTER

Though men are false, God is faithful.

MATTHEW HENRY

The Lord will keep his promises.
With love he takes care of all he has made.

PSALM 145:13 NCV

Kindness

Always try to be kind to each other.

1 Thessalonians 5:15 nlt

KINDNESS is not always soft, quiet, and cuddly. Sometimes it boldly speaks the words someone needs to hear. It stands up for what's right, even when what's right isn't what's popular. Kindness does whatever it takes to do what's in the best interest of another.

What gives kindness its gentle strength is love. Every word and action, whether meeting the physical needs of a stranger or confronting a friend on her tendency toward unhealthy behaviors, is motivated by other-centered compassion. Kindness is sensitive to different personality types, creatively crafting an appropriate response for each unique situation. It always leaves pride and judgment behind and reaches out with open, accepting arms to tenderly help another move closer to God. How can you put kindness into action today?

~~~~~~~~~~~~~~~~~~~~~~~~~~~~~

A kind heart is a fountain of gladness, making everything in its vicinity freshen into smiles.

Washington Irving

Constant kindness can accomplish much.
As the sun makes ice melt, kindness causes
misunderstanding, mistrust and
hostility to evaporate.

ALBERT SCHWEITZER

Be the living expression of God's kindness:
kindness in your face, kindness in your eyes,
kindness in your smile,
kindness in your warm greeting.

MOTHER TERESA

Be kind. Remember that everyone you meet
is fighting a hard battle.

HARRY THOMPSON

As God's chosen people, holy and dearly loved,
clothe yourselves with compassion, kindness,
humility, gentleness and patience.

COLOSSIANS 3:12 NIV

Peace

You, LORD, give perfect peace to those who keep
their purpose firm and put their trust in you.

ISAIAH 26:3 GNT

A S EVERY beauty-pageant contestant seems
to agree, peace—world peace—is one of
the deepest desires of the human heart. But what's
less frequently understood is that peace is not
determined by location or situation. Peace will
blanket the world only when Jesus Christ is Lord of
all nations and every heart is surrendered to Him.

War, relational conflict, and inner turmoil are
all part of life on this earth. But that doesn't mean
you can't have perfect peace in your own heart. It's
available right now. Ask God to give you a taste of
what true peace is like, as you trust in His goodness
and rest in His presence.

~~~~~~~~~~~~~~~~~~~~~~~~~~~~~

If the basis of peace is God,
the secret of peace is trust.

<div align="right">

J. N. FIGGIS

</div>

No God, no peace. Know God, know peace.

AUTHOR UNKNOWN

Christ alone can bring lasting peace—
peace with God—peace among men
and nations—and peace within our hearts.

BILLY GRAHAM

Peace rules the day when Christ rules the mind.

AUTHOR UNKNOWN

*God's peace will keep your hearts and minds
in Christ Jesus. The peace that God gives
is so great that we cannot understand it.*

PHILIPPIANS 4:7 NCV

Guidance

If I ride the morning winds to the farthest oceans,
even there your hand will guide me,
your strength will support me.

PSALM 139:9–10 TLB

A GLOBAL Positioning System would be a great graduation gift. You could type in your goals—where you want to go—and a friendly voice would advise you as to the best way to get there.

Your relationship with God is better than any GPS on the market. God knows where you've been, where you are, and which direction is best for you to head in the future. God wants you to have access to that same useful information. By reading the Bible, weighing advice from godly friends, and asking God's Spirit to guide you in prayer, you have access to a system of guidance that will never fail, no matter where you roam.

~~~~~~~~~~~~~~~~~~~~~~~~~~~~~~

When we fail to wait prayerfully for God's guidance and strength, we are saying with our actions, if not our lips, that we do not need him.

CHARLES HUMMEL

I know not the way God leads me,
but well do I know my Guide.

MARTIN LUTHER

Deep in your heart it is not guidance
that you want as much as a guide.

JOHN WHITE

The teacher of teachers gives his guidance
noiselessly. I have never heard him speak,
and yet I know that he is within me.
At every moment he instructs me and guides me.
And whenever I am in need of it,
he enlightens me afresh.

THERESE OF LISIEUX

Lord, tell me your ways. Show me how to live.
Guide me in your truth.

PSALM 25:4–5 NCV

Fellowship

If we are living in the light of God's presence, just as Christ is, then we have fellowship with one another.
1 JOHN 1:7 NLT

FELLOWSHIP is an old-fashioned-sounding word, bringing to mind potlucks—complete with fat-laden casseroles and colorful gelatin salads—eaten in church basement fellowship halls. But true fellowship is never out of date. It's people living on the cutting edge of community, sharing life together.

When Christ is the center of that life, the common bond is more than friendship. It's a love that matures through differences and struggle, as well as through praise and play.

To experience fellowship, you have to involve your life with the lives of other people who believe in Christ. You need to risk being real and work your way through problems, instead of running from them. Only then can you experience the joy that being part of God's family brings.

~~~~~~~~~~~~~~~~~~~~~~~~~~~~

Be united with other Christians.
A wall with loose bricks is not good.
The bricks must be cemented together.
CORRIE TEN BOOM

The only basis for real fellowship with God
and man is to live out in the open with both.

ROY HESSION

The virtuous soul that is alone and without
a master is like a lone burning coal;
it will grow colder rather than hotter.

JOHN OF THE CROSS

No man is an island, entire of itself;
every man is a piece of the continent,
a part of the main.

JOHN DONNE

Do not be interested only in your own life,
but be interested in the lives of others.

PHILIPPIANS 2:4 NCV

Identity

*The Spirit himself joins with out spirits
to say that we are God's children.*

ROMANS 8:16 NCV

WAY back in the sixties, young adults were obsessed with "finding themselves." To accomplish this, they experimented with things like drugs, communal living, and transcendental meditation. Unfortunately, these are ways to *lose* yourself.

What was true in the sixties is true today. There's only one way to find your true identity—believe what God has to say about you. God says you're loved, forgiven, unique, and eternally significant. As His child, you're also part of a new family that is destined to make a positive impact on this world and the next.

Take a moment to thank God for the many ways He's helping you "find yourself" in Him.

~~~~~~~~~~~~~~~~~~~~~~~~~~~~

He who counts the stars and calls them
by their names is in no danger of forgetting
His own children.

CHARLES HADDON SPURGEON

The way in which we think of ourselves
has everything to do with how
our world sees us.

ARLENE RAVEN

Is it a small thing in your eyes to be loved
by God—to be the son, the spouse,
the love, the delight of the King of glory?

RICHARD BAXTER

Everything is good when it leaves
the Creator's hands.

JEAN-JACQUES ROUSSEAU

*Put on the new man which was created according
to God, in true righteousness and holiness.*

EPHESIANS 4:24 NKJV

Protection

*The LORD your God will lead you
and protect you on every side.*

ISAIAH 52:12 GNT

YOU can eat your vegetables, wear your seat belt, always hike with a buddy, even be a black belt in the martial arts, but there's only one thing that's guaranteed to offer complete protection anytime, anywhere—putting your life fully in God's hands.

That doesn't mean the laws of physics will no longer apply if you drive faster than the speed limit or angels will necessarily do physical battle with would-be muggers who happen to come your way. What it does mean is God will fight for you. He will protect what is most important—your heart and your eternal destiny.

~~~~~~~~~~~~~~~~~~~~~~~~~~~~~~

Safe am I. Safe am I, in the hollow of His hand.

OLD SUNDAY SCHOOL SONG

Prayer is the key that shuts us up under
his protection and safeguard.

JACQUES ELLUL

Those who walk in God's shadow
are not shaken by the storm.

ANDREA GARNEY

This is a wise, sane Christian faith:
that a man commit himself, his life,
and his hopes to God, and that God undertakes
the special protection of that man.

GEORGE MACDONALD

The LORD will keep you from all evil;
he will keep your life. The LORD will keep
your going out and your coming in from
this time on and forevermore.

PSALM 121:7–8 NRSV

Influence

*Provide people with a glimpse of good living
and of the living God.*

PHILIPPIANS 2:15 THE MESSAGE

YOU are a walking, talking message of hope. Whether you realize it or not, your character, words, and actions are all preaching a sermon to those you meet along the road of life. The closer you follow God, the more visible He'll be to others through you.

You may never know how wide your influence really goes. An act of kindness, a word of encouragement, or a job well done could be what moves a close friend, or even a stranger, one step closer to knowing God.

Take a moment to thank God for the people who've had a positive influence on your life. Then, ask God to help you become someone else's reason for thanks.

~~~~~~~~~~~~~~~~~~~~~~~~~~~~

Immortality lies not in the things you leave behind, but in the people your life has touched.

AUTHOR UNKNOWN

We can influence others as much as
God has influenced us.

BOBBIE-JEAN MERCK

The most important single influence in the life of
a person is another person ...
who is worthy of emulation.

PAUL D. SHAFER

Example is not the main thing
in influencing others.
It is the only thing.

ALBERT SCHWEITZER

Be ready to give a defense to everyone who asks
you a reason for the hope that is in you,
with meekness and fear.

1 PETER 3:15

Thankfulness

Whatever happens, keep thanking God because of Jesus Christ. This is what God wants you to do.

1 THESSALONIANS 5:18 CEV

YOU don't need a turkey to celebrate Thanksgiving. All you need is a reason. God has given you more reasons to be thankful than He's created stars in the sky. So, why wait?

Start with what you see ... the clothes you're wearing, the food in the fridge, the beauty of a summer day. Then, think about the people you love and how they've touched your life. Next, consider what God's given you that can't be held in your hands—things like hope, forgiveness, and your future home in heaven. Sit quietly as God brings even more reasons to mind.

Stopping to say thanks will remind you of how big God is and how good your life is, no matter what kind of day you're having.

~~~~~~~~~~~~~~~~~~~~~~~~~~~~

No duty is more urgent than that of returning thanks.

SAINT AMBROSE

Thanksgiving is good but thanks-living is better.

MATTHEW HENRY

Thanksgiving is the end of all human conduct,
whether observed in words or works.

J. B. LIGHTFOOT

Thou has given so much to me.
Give me one thing more—a grateful heart.

GEORGE HERBERT

Everything God made is good, and nothing
should be refused if it is accepted with thanks.

1 TIMOTHY 4:4 NCV

Faithfulness

The LORD preserves the faithful.

PSALM 31:24 NIV

GOD will never waver in His faithfulness toward you. But faithfulness is not a quality reserved for deity. With God's help, you can be faithful in your relationships with others, as well as with Him.

Just look to Him as your example. Ask yourself, "How would God treat this person?" or "What decision would most likely make God smile?" Whatever your answer, it involves some aspect of God's faithfulness.

When your promises can be trusted, your commitments can be depended upon, and your friends know they can rely on you to be devoted and true, you're faithfully walking in God's own footsteps.

~~~~~~~~~~~~~~~~~~~~~~~~~~~~~~

God did not call us to be successful,
but to be faithful.

MOTHER TERESA

We know that our reward depends not on
the job itself but on the faithfulness
with which we serve God.

JOHN PAUL I

Faithfulness in little things is a big thing.

SAINT JOHN CHRYSOSTOM

He does most in God's great world who does
his best in his own little world.

THOMAS JEFFERSON

Do not let loyalty and faithfulness forsake you;
bind them around your neck,
write them on the tablet of your heart.

PROVERBS 3:3 NRSV

Life

*Your life is a journey that you must travel
with a deep consciousness of God.*

1 PETER 1:17 THE MESSAGE

WHAT is the meaning of life? This question has been debated by philosophy classes for centuries. But guess what? You know the answer. Life is a journey toward, or away from, the heart of God. Keeping that in mind makes even the most ordinary day seem extraordinarily important. And it is.

What you do with today matters. Whether you're riding roller coasters with friends or feeding the hungry at a soup kitchen doesn't matter as much as whether what you're doing is drawing you closer to, or farther away from, the One who loves you most.

Where will life take you today? The direction is up to you.

~~~~~~~~~~~~~~~~~~~~~~~~~~~~~~

I will not just live my life.
I will not just spend my life. I will invest my life.

HELEN KELLER

Let God have your life;
he can do more with it than you can.

DWIGHT L. MOODY

Life is a great big canvas;
throw all the paint on it you can.

DANNY KAYE

The value of life lies not in the length of days,
but in the use we make of them.

MICHEL DE MONTAIGNE

He that findeth his life shall lose it:
and he that loseth his life for my sake shall find it.

MATTHEW 10:39 KJV

Strength

The LORD is my strength and my shield.

PSALM 28:7 NIV

IF YOU want to strengthen your muscles, you work out. You lift weights, increasing your repetitions as time goes by. The same is true for building up your spiritual muscles. As God trusts you with increasingly heavier responsibility and you choose to rely on Him more and more, you'll be able to stand stronger, longer—no matter what the circumstances.

The next time you feel weak or afraid, don't believe what you feel. Listen to what God has to say. Rely on the knowledge you've been working out with your very own Personal Trainer. God knows just the right exercises to help turn your weaknesses into strengths.

~~~~~~~~~~~~~~~~~~~~~~~~~~~~~

God ... is not in the business of helping
the humanly strong become stronger;
rather he takes the weak
and makes them strong in himself.

ERWIN W. LUTZER

The Lord doesn't promise to give us something to
take so we can handle our weary moments.
He promises us himself. That is all.
And that is enough.

CHARLES R. SWINDOLL

The weaker we feel, the harder we lean on God.
And the harder we lean, the stronger we grow.

JONI EARECKSON TADA

When God is our strength, it is strength indeed;
when our strength is our own, it is only weakness.

SAINT AUGUSTINE OF HIPPO

*I can do all things through Christ because
he gives me strength.*

PHILIPPIANS 4:13 NCV

Mercy

What does the LORD require of you?
To act justly and to love mercy
and to walk humbly with your God.

MICAH 6:8 NIV

MERCY is the key that sets a prisoner free. It extends grace in place of judgment, forgiveness in place of punishment, honor in place of disdain. It makes no sense, except to a heart filled with God's unconditional love.

Mercy is a gift God asks you to give to others— not because they deserve it, but because of the mercy God has demonstrated in your own life. Ask God to bring to mind anyone who could use a tender touch of mercy. Depending on how God leads you to bestow this special gift, the one who receives it may never even be fully aware of its extent. But you will. You'll find that being merciful frees up your own heart to love more authentically.

~~~~~~~~~~~~~~~~~~~~~~~~~~~~~

Nothing graces the Christian soul
as much as mercy.

<div align="right">SAINT AMBROSE</div>

Mercy is compassion in action.

AUTHOR UNKNOWN

He who demands mercy and shows none ruins
the bridge over which he himself is to pass.

THOMAS ADAMS

Two works of mercy set a man free: forgive
and you will be forgiven,
and give and you will receive.

SAINT AUGUSTINE OF HIPPO

Jesus said, "Blessed are the merciful,
for they will be shown mercy."

MATTHEW 5:7 NIV

Commitment

Commit everything you do to the Lord.

PSALM 37:5 TLB

GOD is committed to you. He won't bail on His promises or put you on "prayer waiting" because a more important call has come in. He will do what He says.

Before you make a commitment, whether to a relationship, a job, or even to volunteer to sell donuts at church on Sunday mornings, you need to weigh the cost. Ask yourself if your time, energy, resources, and talents are all at a level where you can follow through on your promise. Ask God to help you make commitments that fit with His purpose and direction for your life.

Then, make one more commitment. Commit whatever you're doing to God. Through success, failure, struggles, and growth, allow Him to help you keep your word.

~~~~~~~~~~~~~~~~~~~~~~~~~~~~~

Unless commitment is made, there are only promises and hope ... but no plans.

PETER DRUCKER

He who lightly assents will seldom
keep his word.

CHINESE PROVERB

If you deny yourself commitment,
what can you do with your life?

HARVEY FIERSTEIN

The moment one definitely commits oneself,
the Providence moves too. All sorts of things
occur to help that would never
otherwise have occurred.

W. H. MURRAY

LORD, *who may dwell in your sanctuary?*
Who may live on your holy hill?
He ... who keeps his oath even when it hurts.

PSALM 15:1, 4 NIV

God's Forgiveness

You forgive us, so that we should stand in awe of you.
PSALM 130:4 GNT

IMAGINE receiving a gift so overly generous that it leaves you speechless. You've done nothing to earn it. As a matter of fact, at times you've been downright awful to the one who's giving it to you. How does your heart respond?

The forgiveness of God is just such a gift. Your response to that gift, whether you apologize for the past and accept it joyfully with open arms or you bury your head in shame and refuse to take what you don't deserve, is your gift to God. Which will it be?

Right now, kneel before the Giver of all good gifts. Meditate on what He's forgiven in your life and what it cost for Him to offer that free gift to you.

~~~~~~~~~~~~~~~~~~~~~~~~~~~~~~~

Forgiveness does not mean the cancellation of all consequences of wrongdoing.
It means the refusal on God's part to let our guilty past affect His relationship with us.
AUTHOR UNKNOWN

There is only one person God cannot forgive:
the one who refuses to come to him
for forgiveness.

AUTHOR UNKNOWN

I think that if God forgives us,
we must forgive ourselves.

C. S. LEWIS

The most marvelous ingredient in the forgiveness
of God is that he also forgets—the one thing
a human being can never do.

OSWALD CHAMBERS

You, Lord, are good, and ready to forgive.
PSALM 86:5

Wealth

My God will use his wonderful riches
in Christ Jesus to give you everything you need.

PHILIPPIANS 4:19 NCV

YOUR diploma is your ticket to a higher income bracket. But no matter what your future net worth winds up to be, you're rich. You found true wealth the moment you chose to follow God, instead of your own prideful heart.

Whether you choose to enjoy the abundance of those riches or bury that eternal treasure and continue striving for the kind of wealth you can hold in your hands, will determine how much you enjoy life—and God.

Consider the priceless riches you possess—love, joy, peace, and hope, to mention just a few. No amount of money can buy treasures like these. Enjoy what you've been given by nurturing a thankful heart. Then, share the wealth by pointing others to God's true treasure.

~~~~~~~~~~~~~~~~~~~~~~~~~~~~~

The real measure of our wealth is how much
we'd be worth if we lost all our money.

<div align="right">JOHN HENRY JOWETT</div>

There is nothing wrong with people
possessing riches. The wrong comes
when riches possess people.

BILLY GRAHAM

If you want to feel rich, just count all
the things you have that money can't buy.

AUTHOR UNKNOWN

God only and not wealth, maintains the world.

MARTIN LUTHER

Command those who are rich in this present age
not to ... trust in uncertain riches but in
the living God, who gives us richly all things to enjoy.

1 TIMOTHY 6:17

Goals

*It's in Christ that we find out who we are
and what we are living for.*

Ephesians 1:12 The Message

ONCE upon a time, your goal was to graduate. You set your sights on a date, figured out what was required of you, then set mini-goals for completing every individual assignment along the way. Step-by-step you made it to where you wanted to be.

To meet a goal of any kind, you need to have a concrete understanding of what it requires—and of who you are. God can help you do just that. Let Him help you evaluate potential goals that lie ahead and see how they fit with who He created you to be. Then, prioritize the steps it will take to reach your goal in a way that honors Him.

~~~~~~~~~~~~~~~~~~~~~~~~~~~~~

The tragedy in life doesn't lie in not reaching your goal. The tragedy lies in having no goal to reach.

Benjamin Mays

You become successful the moment you start
moving toward a worthwhile goal.

AUTHOR UNKNOWN

First build a proper goal. That proper goal
will make it easy, almost automatic,
to build a proper you.

JOHANN WOLFGANG VON GOETHE

The goal of a virtuous life is to become like God.

GREGORY OF NYSSA

Our only goal is to please God.

2 CORINTHIANS 5:9 NCV

Eternal Life

When people sin, they earn what sin pays—death.
But God gives us a free gift—
life forever in Christ Jesus our Lord.

ROMANS 6:23 NCV

YOUR life will not end with a death certificate. God has made that null and void. There's true life ahead, at a deeper and more beautiful level than anything you can possibly experience in this world broken by sin.

Life on Earth is really just the beginning. It's like the childhood of your eternity. Today's your chance to grow and learn, to get acquainted with God and His creations, to get a small, inviting taste of what's to come.

Take hold of today with your whole heart. Enjoy it. Explore it. Give yourself fully toward living it well. But never lose sight of eternity. There's so much more to living and real life than what you can see from where you stand right now.

~~~~~~~~~~~~~~~~~~~~~~~~~~~~~

Eternity to the godly is a day that has no sunset.

THOMAS WATSON

Eternity is the place where questions
and answers become one.

ELI WIESSEL

People who dwell in God dwell
in the Eternal Now.

MEISTER ECKHART

The life of faith does not earn eternal life;
it is eternal life. And Christ is its vehicle.

WILLIAM TEMPLE

Whoever believes in the Son has eternal life.

JOHN 3:36 NRSV

Meditation

I will think about your miracles.

PSALM 145:5 NCV

MEDITATION gets a bad rap. It gets tied in with the New Age movement, Eastern religion, even weight-loss programs. But way back in Old Testament times, God told people to meditate. The key was what He told them to meditate on—Him.

Meditating on God—His character, His miracles, and His words as communicated in the Bible—helps you understand more about what God is really like. It helps change your thinking and even your behavior, from the inside out.

Set aside five uninterrupted minutes today to mediate on God. Choose one quality of God's character and think about the difference it makes in your life. Let it lead you to thanks, to praise, and closer to the heart of God Himself.

~~~~~~~~~~~~~~~~~~~~~~~~~~~~~

In the rush and noise of life, as you have intervals, step home within yourselves and be still.
Wait upon God, and feel his good presence; this will carry you evenly through your day's business.

WILLIAM PENN

Those who draw water from the wellspring of
meditation know that God dwells
close to their hearts.

TOYOHIKO KAGAWA

Let us leave the surface and, without leaving
the world, plunge into God.

TEILHARD DE CHARDIN

Meditation is the activity of calling to mind,
and thinking over, and dwelling on,
and applying to oneself, the various things
that one knows about the works and ways
and purposes and promises of God.

J. I. PACKER

*Let the words of my mouth and the meditation of
my heart be acceptable in Your sight, O LORD,
my strength and my Redeemer.*

PSALM 19:14

Hope

We hope for something we have not yet seen,
and we patiently wait for it.

ROMANS 8:25 CEV

HOPE is the perfect life preserver in the midst of any storm. It helps keep your head above water, enabling you to fight off feelings of discouragement and despair. As you catch an occasional glimpse of what lies beyond the waves, it aids in reminding you that help is on the way, even if you can't quite see it yet. Hope helps you survive.

When storm clouds are gathering on the horizon, or if a torrential downpour has caught you by surprise, hold fast to hope. Remember how God came through time and time again for people in the Bible. Think about how He's come through for you. Then, meditate on His steadfast promises, your greatest source of hope. Help is on its way.

~~~~~~~~~~~~~~~~~~~~~~~~~~~~~

There is no better or more blessed bondage
than to be a prisoner of hope.

ROY Z. KEMP

There is no medicine like hope, no incentive
so great, and no tonic so powerful
as expectation of something tomorrow.

SAMUEL JOHNSON

What oxygen is to the lungs, such is hope for
the meaning of life.

HEINRICH EMIL BRUNNER

Do not look to your hope, but to Christ,
the source of your hope.

CHARLES HADDON SPURGEON

May the God of hope fill you with all joy and peace
as you trust in him, so that you may overflow
with hope by the power of the Holy Spirit.

ROMANS 15:13 NIV

Faith

*Let us draw near to God with a sincere heart
in full assurance of faith.*

HEBREWS 10:22 NIV

FAITH is trust that's put to the test. It acts on what it believes to be true. If you have faith your best friend can keep a secret, you'll risk being honest about your biggest mistakes and regrets. If you have faith God really loves you, you'll risk making a decision you believe will honor Him, even if it promises not to be easy.

Faith grows the more you use it, the more you try it on for size. Give God the chance to grow yours. Act on what He's asked you to do. Risk moving out of your comfort level. Do more than believe with your heart. Move forward in faith, wherever He's leading you to go.

~~~~~~~~~~~~~~~~~~~~~~~~~~~~~

Faith is the final meaning of human existence,
and the answers to the questions on which
all our happiness depends cannot be found
in any other way.

THOMAS MERTON

As the flower is before the fruit,
so is faith before good works.

RICHARD WHATELY

The act of faith is more than a bare statement
of belief; it is a turning to the face
of the living God.

CHRISTOPHER BRYANT

Faith is to believe what you do not yet see:
the reward for this faith
is to see what you believe.

SAINT AUGUSTINE OF HIPPO

We walk by faith, not by sight.

2 CORINTHIANS 5:7 NRSV

Contentment

I have learned to be satisfied with the things I have and with everything that happens.

How much is enough? To a contented heart, it's as much as God has chosen to provide. To measure your personal level of contentment, complete this sentence: I would be content if only...

What are the "if onlys" in your life? More money? Being involved in a serious relationship? Losing or gaining weight? Landing the job of your dreams?

There's another name for "if onlys." They're called idols. When your desires move from "it would be nice" to "I can't be happy without," you've chosen to believe some *thing* can satisfy you, instead of Someone. Ask God to reveal any "if onlys" you need to confront. Then, ask Him to show you how to find contentment where you are, and with what you have, right now.

~~~~~~~~~~~~~~~~~~~~~~~~~~~~~~

God is most glorified in us when we
are most satisfied in him.

JOHN PIPER

A little is as much as a lot, if it is enough.

STEVE BROWN

The utmost we can hope for in this life
is contentment.

JOSEPH ADDISON

The secret of contentment is the realization
that life is a gift, not a right.

AUTHOR UNKNOWN

Do you want to be truly rich?
You already are if you are happy and good.

1 TIMOTHY 6:6 TLB

Character

Jesus said, "Your task is to be true, not popular."
LUKE 6:26 THE MESSAGE

YOUR character is who you are when no one's watching. It's the very best of you, and worst of you, all rolled into one. One of the goals of maturing is to get your character in line with who God created you to be.

Though there is no one quite like you, there are qualities your character should share with all those who follow God. Traits such as honesty, integrity, generosity, and deep-hearted love should be an essential part of who you are and how you relate in this life as God's child.

But, character develops out of choice, not chance. Choose to work on erasing any traits that don't reflect God's own character. Ask for God's help in developing the qualities most like His own.

~~~~~~~~~~~~~~~~~~~~~~~~~~~~~

Reputation is what men and women think of us.
Character is what God and the angels know of us.
THOMAS PAINE

Character is not in the mind. It is in the will.

FULTON JOHN SHEEN

Character—the sum of those qualities that
make a man a good man
and a woman a good woman.

THEODORE ROOSEVELT

Character is what you are in the dark.

DWIGHT L. MOODY

Endurance produces character,
and character produces hope.

ROMANS 5:4 NRSV

Priorities

*I want you to do whatever will help you serve
the Lord best, with as few distractions as possible.*

1 CORINTHIANS 8:35 NLT

How you live your life reflects your true priorities more than any list you may be holding in your head. Suppose your love for others is evident to those who know you—and even those who don't. Suppose you talk to God about both the small things as well as the big ones you face each and every day. And suppose you make plans for your future based on the big picture of eternity, instead of the small snapshot of daily life. Then, chances are, you're trying to keep God number one in your life.

That isn't something you decide once and then forget. Every morning you need to make a choice ... "Who will be number one in my life, God or me?"

~~~~~~~~~~~~~~~~~~~~~~~~~~~~~

Tell me to what you pay attention,
and I will tell you who you are.

JOSÉ ORTEGA Y GASSET

When first things are put first, second things
are not suppressed but increased.

C. S. LEWIS

When you put God first, you are establishing
order for everything else in your life.

ANDREA GARNEY

Do not let the good things in life rob you
of the best things.

BUSTER ROTHMAN

*Jesus said, "It is worth nothing for a man to have
the whole world if he loses his soul."*

MATTHEW 16:26 NCV

Heaven

*He puts a little of heaven in our hearts
so that we'll never settle for less.*

2 CORINTHIANS 5:5 THE MESSAGE

GRADUATION day is a combination of ceremony, excitement, endings, and brand-new beginnings. It's a celebration that's hard to forget. But there's another graduation day ahead, one you may be a little more hesitant to participate in. That's the day you graduate to life after death.

It's a little unnerving not knowing what to expect. But one thing is certain. God's been waiting for that day with greater expectation than you had about saying good-bye to your toughest class. He's prepared a place just for you, a place where you truly belong.

Anytime the fear of death grabs hold of your heart, just picture meeting God face-to-face and hearing Him say with a smile, "Welcome home!"

~~~~~~~~~~~~~~~~~~~~~~~~~~~~~

Earth has no sorrow that heaven cannot heal.

THOMAS V. MOORE

Heaven is a prepared place for a prepared people.
LEWIS SPERRY CHAFER

Heaven will be the perfection we have
always longed for. All the things that made earth
unlovely and tragic will be absent in heaven.
BILLY GRAHAM

God's retirement plan is out of this world.
AUTHOR UNKNOWN

Our bodies are like tents that we live in here on earth.
But when these tents are destroyed, we know that
God will give each of us a place to live. These homes
will not be buildings that someone has made,
but they are in heaven and will last forever.
2 CORINTHIANS 5:1 CEV

Future

Continue to reverence the Lord all the time,
for surely you have a wonderful future ahead of you.

PROVERBS 23:18 TLB

Y OU can only grab hold of the future one day at a time. The rest of it's out of your reach. That doesn't mean you can't look forward to it, plan for it, or even daydream a bit about it. But the future's like a movie preview of coming attractions. You're only allowed a glimpse of what's to come. The real draw is the main attraction, what's ready for you to experience here and now.

Today is your main attraction, so use it in a way that draws you closer to God. You'll assure yourself of a brighter future—one destined to make a blockbuster of an impact on those around you and ensure you of a happily ever after with the One you love.

~~~~~~~~~~~~~~~~~~~~~~~~~~~~~

Never be afraid to trust an unknown future
to a known God.

CORRIE TEN BOOM

The only light on the future is faith.

THEODOR HOECKER

I've read the last page of the Bible.
It's all going to turn out all right.

BILLY GRAHAM

The future is as bright as the promises of God.

ADONIRAM JUDSON

The Lord's plans will stand forever.
His ideas will last from now on.

PSALM 33:11 NCV

Topical Index

Additional copies of this book
and other titles from ELM HILL PRESS
are available from your local bookstore.

Other titles in this series:

God's Daily Answer
God's Daily Answer for Teachers
God's Daily Answer for Women
God's Daily Answer for Men
God's Daily Answer for Mothers
God's Daily Answer Devotional